The Essence of Acting: Techniques, Triumphs, and Trials

Lloyd Green

Published by Lloyd Green, 2023.

THE ESSENCE OF ACTING: TECHNIQUES, TRIUMPHS, AND TRIALS

First edition. November 4, 2023.

ISBN: 979-8223048886

Written by Lloyd Green.

Also by Lloyd Green

The Prepper's Ultimate Guide: Building Sustainable Shelters for
Long-Term Survival
Original Six Era: The Rise of the Chicago Blackhawks Dynasty
Legends of the Diamond: The New York Yankees' Timeless Tale
The First Kiss Blueprint: Steps to a Moment She'll Never Forget
The Essence of Acting: Techniques, Triumphs, and Trials

Table of Contents

The Essence of Acting: Techniques, Triumphs, and Trials

History of Acting by Elizabeth Jewell

Instructor Elizabeth Jewell examines the main periods in acting history. This includes Greek theatre development, church processionals contribution to theatre performance, commedia dell'arte performances of 17th Century English comedy as well as Shakespeare.

She goes on to explain that male actors often wore feminine-style costumes when portraying female roles, leading them down the path of Method Acting.

Ancient Greek Theatre

Ancient Greece saw the world's first recorded theatre performance around 600 BCE during religious festivals honoring Dionysus. According to legend, Thespis a wandering bard won a contest at City Dionysia by leaping onto a wooden cart and performing poetry as though he were performing for characters he read from, thus becoming known as its first actor and thus becoming history's first actor.

Greek plays of this era were frequently inspired by stories from Greek mythology and should not be taken literally. Instead, we can attribute comedy and tragedy performances with masks representing Thalia (Muse of Comedy) and Melpomeme (Muse of Tragedy) - two muses from Greek mythology who helped inspire these genres of entertainment.

Ancient Greece enjoyed an immense love affair with theatre. Three playwrights in particular gained prominence during this era - Aeschylus, Sophocles and Euripides. Aeschylus introduced innovative concepts like adding second actors for staged tragedies; breaking trilogie cycles by adding painted scenery. Sophocles and Euripides earned praise for their clever dialogues as well as thought-provoking treatment of familiar themes in their plays.

Producing and performing a Greek tragedy was no simple task; it required years of hard work from actors. Reciting lines slowly in a low voice while wearing heavy costumes covered their heads was no simple task either; scenes took place in an orchestrated performance space with half-moon seats known as the skene for added drama.

The Renaissance

The Renaissance brought with it a dramatic transformation in art and culture. Painters and sculptors gave society a whole new view of beauty that still resonates today in our contemporary forms of art - theatre was no exception to this shift in thinking.

At this time, theatre saw its revival through various means. One significant development was the formation of acting companies - groups of young men who rented or built their own theatre and shared its profits after hosting performances.

Another major development during this era was the rise of comedy as an artistic form; these plays featured improvised elements based on Satyr and Pastoral plays. Finally, another key development occurred with opera, an amalgam of music and theatre which continues today.

Actors were also forced to adapt to numerous social changes that affected theatre during this period, particularly those brought on by religious opposition to theatrical performances. Church authorities worked tirelessly against their influence; actors were seen as potentially dangerous people like Gypsies or Homosexuals who should be persecuted for performing onstage.

At this time, society experienced another major transformation with the end of feudalism and rise of market economies. Due to the Black Death's creation of middle classes and people trading goods more freely. Due to these developments, professional actors became essential who could speak effectively in front of an audience.

The Age of Enlightenment

The Age of Enlightenment, also referred to as the Scientific Revolution and Age of Reason, was an influential European social movement from late seventeenth century until early nineteenth century that promoted intellectual advancement alongside an emphasis on liberalism and progressivism.

The philosophy of the Age of Enlightenment revolved around a desire to better understand nature and human behavior through science. Additionally, this movement highlighted empiricism and rational thought while viewing religious dogma and traditional beliefs as obstacles to progress.

Literature of the Enlightenment period often employed satire and mockery as its signature tactics. Perhaps most famous from this era is John Milton's epic poem Paradise Lost, which tells the Biblical tale of Adam and Eve's fall from grace. Alexander Pope also popularized satirical poetry during this era; one such work from him is The Rape of the Lock (1712) where exaggeration and hyperbole are used to compare everyday arguments between two suitors to epic battles depicted in classical Greek mythologies.

The Age of Enlightenment can also be seen as having played an essential part in Western political modernization, due to its influence on liberal politics such as church-state separation, egalitarian thought and interpretations of laws with no interference by religious authorities.

The Age of Romanticism

Romanticism was a global movement that swept across Europe during the late 18th and early 19th centuries, challenging the rational ideals held so closely during Enlightenment. Romanticism's ideals of emotion over reason fueled avant-garde movements into the 20th century while simultaneously helping redefine our concept of vision and how we see our world today.

Romanticism has often been associated with themes of love and desire; however, its scope was far wider. Romantic artists sought to convey a range of emotions through naturalistic imagery. Additionally, many turned to past eras for inspiration like medieval or Renaissance art - Edward Burne-Jones and Dante Gabriel Rosetti were two British Pre-Raphaelite painters who depicted Medieval, religious, and Shakespearean scenes through Romantic sensibilities.

John Keats was one of the best-known literary poets of Romanticism and used emotive language to portray intense feelings of love and loss through his odes, which focused on natural imagery. Romanticism also contained elements of rebellion; Gericault's Raft of Medusa (1818-19) criticizes government policies which contributed to shipwrecks while Turner's The Slave Ship (1840) intended to hasten its abolition.

The Age of Industrialization

The Industrial Revolution marked a period in history in which our economy transitioned from being predominantly agricultural to one characterized by manufacturing factories, with significant increases in economic output, urban sprawl and rapid changes to transportation and production technologies.

Samuel Slater brought the Spinning Jenny from Britain to Rhode Island in 1789, starting the first textile mill on American soil. By 1861, cotton mills had spread far and wide, replacing agricultural work with wage labor. Industrialization enabled railroad construction and hastened commerce; cities expanded quickly while tenements filled up quickly as people looked for employment. Industrialization also brought with it "robber barons", wealthy tycoons who built empires through unethical practices.

Industrialization transformed family life as it led to children being sent away to cities as workers, often at such young ages that it reshaped family dynamics. Workers endured long hours and low pay; this led to opposition such as Luddites who violently opposed change; however its benefits are immense and still drive economies worldwide today; regardless of how we measure its effects it's undeniable that Industrial Revolution shaped modern history forever.

The Age of Modernism

Modernism was an artistic movement spurred on by philosophers like Friedrich Nietzsche and Sigmund Freud that challenged traditional ways of thinking while leading to more individualistic forms of art. Modernism also saw various experimental writing techniques emerge such as blended imagery/themes/absurdism/nonlinear narratives/ stream of consciousness (a free flowing internal monologue).

Modernism was propelled forward by artists in the late 1800s when they found greater artistic freedom to explore subjects that interested them rather than simply painting what patrons commissioned them to. Additionally, psychology provided more abstract approaches to understanding human experiences.

Modernist writers' works were marked by disenchantment with culture and an attempt to escape bourgeois proprieties. Modernist authors used literary techniques like free verse poetry or expressive writing that sometimes seemed jagged and fragmentary to achieve this aim;

for instance, Gertrude Stein used her story "Three Lives" to examine how one's real aspirations and emotions could come through on paper based on her studies with psychologist William James who promoted continuous awareness as literary technique.

The Age of Hollywood

Hollywood may be synonymous with glamour and classic movies, but its industry is also notoriously gender unequal. Northwestern University researchers have looked beyond Hollywood glamour to reveal the harsh reality of film production during Hollywood's Golden Age.

Hollywood of the 1920s saw unprecedented dominance from five major studios and iconic actors and actresses, thanks to sound recording technology and color film's invention. Studios could create larger and more ambitious movies thanks to these innovations - leading to some unforgettable cinematic moments that stand the test of time.

Humphrey Bogart, Marilyn Monroe and Laurence Olivier were admired for their ability to portray diverse roles. Unfortunately, as with everything good that came before it, this era came to a close eventually.

The Supreme Court's 1948 ruling that movie studios could no longer own theaters and only show their films signaled the end of Hollywood's Golden Age. Movie companies were no longer required to release so many movies at one time; instead they became more selective as to which ones would make an appearance in theaters - giving rise to bankable stars that could lead a movie to success at the box office and more creative freedom for directors who sought to develop their unique artistic styles.

The Actor's Instrument

The Actor's Instrument is a phrase that is frequently used in Meisner acting classes. It encompasses the different aspects of an actor's ability to express himself and can be broken down into six broad categories: Physical expression, Intelligence, Imagination, Emotion, Sensory Expression and Empathy.

Rami Malek spent hours every day working on his instrument to be prepared to play Freddie Mercury in the film Bohemian Rhapsody. He worked to strengthen his body, voice, and mind.

Body

In the same way that a painter's brushes and canvass are their tools, an actor's body is his instrument. A successful performance requires a body that can express the character's emotions, needs and journey in a variety of situations. A great actor can use his body to communicate a wide range of emotions and create characters that are real, authentic and believable.

A well-trained and maintained physical ability allows an actor to create and experience the world of his character even in a simple gesture or when standing perfectly still on stage. The mastery of the physical expression of the instrument is an act in itself and takes a lifetime to perfect. The ability to train and maintain this aspect of the actor's instrument is something that separates the good from the great actors.

It is important for an actor to learn how to express the emotions and experiences of his character physically, emotionally and mentally. This is a very complex area of acting because it involves many different elements and aspects that must all be brought together at the same time. The acting teacher will often be able to provide the actor with a set of exercises that will help him to access and express these elements.

One of the most difficult areas for an actor is to be able to fully commit to and live through her own experiences on stage, especially the more uncomfortable ones. For example, I once worked with an actress who struggled with feeling vulnerable, exposed and hurt on stage, which was the exact emotion required for her character to feel in the scene. She had a hard time believing that she could actually feel these things while being watched by an audience, and was very inhibited when she did.

This type of inhibiting problem is common to all actors and it can be caused by a variety of factors. Some acting teachers will simply tell the actor to relax and try not to be so nervous, while other acting gurus are able to clearly identify and articulate the causes of these inhibiting feelings and offer the actor effective means of eliminating them.

Voice

Like a piano player who must be able to play any piece of music with the right tone and sound, an actor must be able to use their voice as an instrument for whatever character they are playing. The best way to do this is to train their voice and have it flexible enough to morph into the character they are portraying. This is a skill that can be learned and will greatly improve an actor's range, fabric and truthfulness in their work.

A good showreel for actors will include a selection of demos that showcase their ability to portray various characters and demonstrate the versatility of their acting ability. These demos will usually consist of a variety of different types of performances, including dramatic scenes and comedies. The showreel should also include vocal warm-up exercises that will help reduce strain on the voice during performance and training sessions.

Most acting schools and teachers focus too little on the development of an actor's instrument and spend far too much time suggesting what character might be good for them to play based on their face or body type. The resulting lack of cohesion between the actor and their craft can seriously diminish an actor's joy and effectiveness in their art.

The most successful actors have a deep awareness of their own unique instrument. This includes a knowledge of their physical self, the nature of their voice and imagination. They can then use all of these aspects to create a fully authentic character that resonates with the audience.

Having an understanding of one's instrument allows the actor to explore the deeper layers of their emotions and experiences. It can even lead to a greater sense of personal freedom. For example, the actress mentioned above who experienced a lot of fear, vulnerability and hurt in her life but was unable to express these feelings on stage was able to uncover where these restrictive habits originated from. She then became able to address them in ways that were healthy and freeing for her.

A great deal of the work that is done on The Method involves exploring these deeper emotions, which can be difficult and uncomfortable to do. In this respect, the work of Eric Morris and other reputable teachers of The Method is very valuable as it teaches the actor specific means to address these issues.

Mind

The acting instrument is the actor's body and voice, but it also includes the mind. To fine tune the actor's instrument and maximize its effectiveness, he must have a keen awareness of himself. A highly trained actor knows how to intuitively and insightfully navigate himself emotionally, physically, vocally and psychologically. He also knows how to take risks and utilise mistakes, and how to expand his capacity for creativity.

The actor's ego or mental body can create interference that inhibits the expression of the emotions required by the role. The ego contains defenses such as denial, distrust, projection, rationalization and intellectualization that can keep the actor from accessing his deeper layers of feelings. Chronic muscular tension can also limit the actor's range of emotional expression.

In addition, the actor must be willing to experience the pain of loss and rejection in order to express the emotions that are required by the role. For example, an actress in a scene might feel great anger because of her character's pain and loss. But if she does not trust herself to actually feel that anger, she may only redirect it as fear and stage fright. Her performance will lack the specificity and truth required to leave an impact with the audience.

Actors must train themselves to be more aware of their bodies and minds and how they react in various situations. They can do this by practicing breathing exercises that help them reclaim their power of attention. In addition, they should spend time each day reflecting on their lives and experiences. This will help them to recognize patterns and habits that can stifle their creativity.

Although the field of psychology has been interested in actors and acting since its nascent beginnings, there is a limited amount of empirical work that specifically addresses the actor and his craft. Nevertheless, the research that does exist is invaluable in helping to identify and understand the specific psychological attributes that can be tapped by acting training. Moreover, the research demonstrates that these psychological attributes can be trained and maintained in the actor through a process of rehearsal and practice.

Imagination

Imagination is one of the most important tools an actor has. It is a tool that can be trained and maintained like any other instrument such as a piano or violin. Actors need to be able to re-experience emotions such as rage, vulnerability, elation, passion, enjoyment, comfort and freedom of expression. These feelings are not only crucial to the role but also vital to the actor's life on and off stage. These experiences can help build a new threshold that allows an actor to experience more of the good things in life as well as overcome obstacles such as fear.

Having an imagination that is strong is very important for actors to be able to access their characters' emotional lives onstage. Often times these feelings may be uncomfortable, frightening or unpleasant. However, an actor needs to be able to push through these barriers in order to deliver a powerful and truthful performance. In order to do this, the actor must have a strong sense of self-trust and security in their ability as craftsman and artists.

The acting technique developed by Sanford Meisner called "The Method" sought to address many of the issues that prevented an actor from accessing real responses and behavior in performance. Using exercises such as repetition and the use of "Emotional Recall," an approach that involved using personal emotion from the actor's memories to feed their acting process, Meisner helped the actor break through the barriers to experience and express life on the stage.

Konstantin Stanislavski and later Lee Strasberg were able to grasp the essence of what Meisner was attempting to accomplish. Their work further developed and improved upon the idea of The Method by addressing an additional element of the instrument that had been missing. The idea that the actor could not only use their imagination to re-experience a scene but that they could also use it to create their character's backstory and to inhabit that world fully.

This was an idea that had been around intuitively for centuries prior to the work of Stanislavski and Strasberg. However, unlike other art forms such as painting or dance, there had been no method that trained the actor to effectively leverage their instrument and create a consistent flow of inspired performances.

Acting Techniques

The act of bringing a script to life on screen requires a range of skills and techniques. Actors use these to create believable and truthful performances.

A famed Russian actor, Constantin Stanislavski, developed an approach to acting that heavily influenced contemporary acting methodologies. His method focuses on building a character from the inside out.

Stanislavski's System

Constantin Stanislavski spent his life trying to create the perfect acting system, and although he never succeeded – a lot of what is taught today is in some way based on the techniques he created. Some parts of his system may not work for every actor, but he certainly made a significant contribution to the art form and there are few acting methodologies that don't at least owe him an enormous debt of gratitude.

The system he developed is a series of psycho-techniques that pave the way for actors to transform into their characters and scenes. It's a complete approach to character that includes both psychological and physical aspects of performance. The psychological side of the method is centered on asking acting questions that help an actor understand the nuanced layers of their character in a deeply engrained way. This process is also known as script analysis and is one of the most important aspects of a role for an actor to understand in order to react truthfully on stage.

The Magic If is a central concept in Stanislavski's system and it allows an actor to explore the character and their circumstances on a deeper level. This is a crucial part of the rehearsal process that helps an actor fully discover their character and create the illusion that they are experiencing their scene for the first time. This is what makes a performance truly alive.

Stanislavski's method also teaches actors to use emotional memory to bring their character to life. This technique involves searching their own lives for feelings that can relate to the character they are playing and using those emotions as their starting point. It's a useful tool to have for any actor and it's similar to the method of Uta Hagen.

Method Acting

Method Actors use experiences from their own lives to bring themselves closer to the character they are playing. They focus on recalling sensations associated with the memory and let their emotions flow freely to allow them to become the character they are playing. This allows them to reflect real feelings on screen which is a huge advantage over actors who simply try to fake it.

Method acting is very time-consuming and requires a lot of dedication. It can be difficult for some actors to break out of their role once filming is over, which can cause problems in their personal life. It can also lead to over-the-top performances that lack realism.

Using personal experience in acting can be effective and is encouraged by Lee Strasberg, a pioneer of the Method approach. He suggested that actors use objects from their daily lives to help them feel the character they are portraying, such as a toothbrush or a piece of clothing. He also suggested that actors should behave in a way that is different from their normal self when they are on set, such as being short-tempered when playing an angry character.

Many famous actors use the Method to give a powerful performance. For example, Daniel Day-Lewis never broke character when he played

Christy Brown in My Left Foot, spending eight weeks at a cerebral palsy clinic to research the role. He also lived in poverty and gained or lost weight to create the physical deterioration of his character's condition.

However, some of the more extreme methods used by actors can cross the line between devotion to their craft and bullying. In one take of Meryl Streep's film The Devil Wears Prada, Hoffman yelled insults at her and even physically slapped her without warning, all in the name of getting the necessary emotional reaction from her character.

Meisner Technique

This acting technique emphasises internalising the emotional circumstances of a scene before entering it. This is known as "emotional preparation", and it enables an actor to respond to the moment, rather than thinking of what they're going to say or do. In doing this, they can make the scene feel natural to an audience.

While this style of acting is not as flexible as other methods, it allows an actor to create a more specific backstory for their character before they enter the scene. This can help them to understand the emotions and motivations of their character. It can also help them to become more connected with their scene partner and improve their improvisation skills.

The Meisner technique uses a variety of exercises to train actors to react to each other in real-time. One of these is the repetition exercise, where two actors repeat a phrase back and forth to each other. This helps them to heighten their awareness and sensitivity of each other's emotions and responses, and it trains them to respond with their gut instead of their mind.

Another technique that Meisner used was to encourage his students to be "emotionally full". This is a concept that asks performers to deeply connect with their own emotions and explore what triggers them, so they can tap into this wealth of authentic information when performing. In doing this, they can honour the reality of feeling scared or angry, instead of just putting on a performance that looks like they're faking it.

Many actors who use the Meisner technique have achieved great success in their careers, including old-Hollywood legends such as Grace Kelly and Gregory Peck, and contemporary stars like Sandra Bullock and Amy Schumer. Audiences adore these performers because their facial reactions to the events in scenes seem very realistic and natural, and they don't come across as "phoney" or over-rehearsed.

Chekhov Technique

The Chekhov Technique is a method of acting that helps actors to become more versatile. It focuses on physicality and uses movement and improvisation exercises to help actors develop their characters. It is also based on intuition and the subconscious mind, which allows actors to be more truthful in their performances. It also integrates ideas from other acting techniques, including Stanislavski's and Meisner's.

Like Meisner's approach, Chekhov's involves the use of imagination to evoke emotion. However, it takes it a step further by exploring the emotions of a character through physical gestures. For example, actors can use a "psychological gesture" to express the feelings and desires of their character. This can be very effective when performing a monologue or even in a scene with multiple characters.

Unlike Stanislavski, Chekhov encouraged actors to take risks and explore their imaginations. He believed that the more creative a moment was on stage, the more the audience would be engaged. This approach is largely why many actors love the Chekhov technique.

Michael Chekhov, the nephew of playwright Anton, developed this acting technique and wrote one of the most important books on acting, To the Actor (also known as On the Technique of Acting). The book is full of improvised acting exercises that help actors become more flexible in their work. However, it can be difficult to understand these techniques without a teacher to guide you through them.

The Chekhov technique is a great way for new and experienced actors alike to expand their repertoires. By learning different acting techniques, you can unlock your unique talent and achieve greater success as an actor. Regardless of which technique you choose, it is essential to gain experience with a wide range of them to determine what works best for you and your career goals.

Violent Integration

This is a relatively new acting technique developed by Tim Phillips, which focuses on the idea that violence is a part of life and should be represented in theater. It encourages actors to access their own experiences with violence, which can help them create more realistic performances. However, this method is not for everyone, and it can be difficult to master.

Actors using this technique often create detailed backstories for their characters and learn as much as they can about their character before beginning rehearsals. This helps them feel more connected to the material and allows them to bring a sense of spontaneity to their performance. It also emphasizes the importance of being fully present in the moment, which can be challenging for some actors.

Another well-known acting technique is the Strasberg method, which was created by Lee Strasberg in the 1940s/1950s. This method shares many of the same principles as Stanislavski's, but also stresses the use of "sense memory," which involves accessing an actor's own past experiences to inform their performance.

In 1960, student activists in Greensboro began sit-ins at whites-only lunch counters. The tactic soon spread to other cities, and was endorsed by the NAACP Youth Council. Students endured taunts, arrests, and beatings in their effort to desegregate restaurants and other public accommodations. The protests prompted the National Leadership Conference on Civil Rights to organize a campaign of nonviolent direct action in the South, which included organizing demonstrations, teaching in "Freedom Schools," and registering voters. The campaigns were a significant factor in the enactment of the Civil Rights Act of 1964. But the fight for full integration continues today. The town of Vidor, Texas is still predominantly white, and some residents express a desire to live in separate neighborhoods.

The Importance of Character Development in Acting

A character's backstory is crucial to their development. It can affect how they think, feel, and act. For example, if a character grew up poor, they may have different survival skills than someone who came from wealth. Their speech patterns can also give a clue about their background.

Every character should experience challenges that make them grow and change in some way. These changes are what make them compelling.

Actors

As characters are the main focus of any narrative, actors must take a great deal of time and effort to create and develop their personalities, flaws, and unique traits in order to create and deliver an engaging performance. This character development process has a profound effect on everything from the character's name and physical attributes to their backstory and point of view. The goal of this process is to make the character appear believable and realistic to the audience so they can connect with them emotionally.

One of the first things an actor must do when developing a character is to clearly define their overarching motivations. This is important because it will help the actor design their given circumstances, plot out their character arc, and shape the secondary characters that surround them. For example, if an actor is playing a tyrannical dictator, it would be helpful to understand why they believe the things they do are right and ethical. This will help the actor not condone their actions and instead find a position of impartiality or neutrality to play the character from.

The next step is to research the character thoroughly. This involves learning about their given circumstances, as well as the world they exist in and the historical context of that time period. For example, an actor may have to look up the history of the city their character is from or even the country. They will also need to understand the time period in which their character is set and the cultural or social norms of that time.

For some actors, this will mean connecting with the character on a very deep level. They might even have to live as the character for a day to fully understand their mannerisms, speech patterns, and interactions with others. This can be a fun and creative way to build a character, especially for an actor with a special skillset like boxing or dancing.

Other actors will find a certain type of character they are best at, which is known as a specialty. These actors often find themselves being typecast in that role over and over again, such as Ray Romano on Men of a Certain Age or Tina Fey on 30 Rock. This is an important part of the character development process, because it will help them refine their craft and become masters at creating that particular type of character.

Research

Researchers conduct a wide variety of studies related to complex characters. These can include studies of individual differences, group dynamics, and character education. Some of these studies are longitudinal and may follow individuals into adulthood. Others are experimental and seek to understand how different factors influence a character's development. While some studies focus on specific traits, such as sociopathy or narcissism, the majority of research on character focuses on the moral dimensions of a person's behavior.

A common trait found in many studies is the belief that children are blank slates that can be written on through modeling and reinforcement. This theory has been challenged by a constructivist school of thought, which maintains that children are meaning makers who interpret their experience and select what parts of it to respond to.

Some scholars have attempted to use sports as a way to develop character. They have found that participation in sport can lead to increased achievement and lower drop out rates in high school. Researchers are unsure of the reasons behind these positive outcomes, but one theory is that sports help to develop important qualities like goal setting, time management, delayed gratification, sequential thinking, initiative, and concentration. These qualities are all considered dimensions of performance character, which is a key element in achieving success in both sports and life.

Another area of research that has been conducted is on the role of self-esteem in character formation. Research has shown that individuals who have a strong sense of self-worth and character tend to achieve higher academic grades and demonstrate greater social responsibility. However, this is a complex relationship and it's not clear whether the self-esteem component of character development has a direct effect on the moral components of a person's character.

As more schools adopt the CASEL standards, there is renewed interest in incorporating social and emotional learning into academics. Many of the skills promoted by this approach are also considered character competencies, including empathy, perspective taking, and moral reasoning competency. Increasingly, teachers are looking for guidance on how to incorporate character education into their classrooms.

Backstories

In acting, creating a character requires an in-depth understanding of that person's backstory. This is because a character's present actions are often the result of their past experiences, and understanding those experiences gives actors a deep level of empathy for the characters they portray. This empathy, in turn, allows them to connect with the challenges and triumphs their characters endure – which, ultimately, makes those characters more relatable and compelling.

A character's backstory is their personal history – the web of formative experiences that shapes their desires, fears and motivations. Without this background, a character feels flat and one-dimensional. However, a character's backstory should not overwhelm the story's events or dilute their actions. The key is to spread the details of a character's backstory out over the course of the novel so that readers have a chance to digest it. This method of revealing the past to your reader helps keep backstory from becoming an info dump, and it also ensures that you don't tell a story that isn't logically necessary for your character's arc.

For example, in a scene that takes place after the death of a family member, you could reveal some of your character's backstory during an intense conversation with that relative. By letting your reader know that this event prompted your character to re-evaluate their life and make some major changes, you allow your audience to experience a sense of believability and emotion along with your character.

Another important aspect of character backstory is that it should show that your characters aren't purely good or bad. Backstory that doesn't reflect the complexity of a character's personality is unconvincing and can cause your readers to lose faith in your story's integrity. To avoid this, resist the temptation to paint your character in black and white. Instead, focus on showing that even the most evil characters are driven by their own pain and fears.

Whether you're an experienced writer or just starting out, developing your characters' backstories is essential to your storytelling success. The best plot in the world can't save a story with weak characters that readers don't care about. So take the time to develop your character's backstory – and watch as your story transforms from mediocre to memorable.

Emotional Connection

As an actor, it's your job to create and develop emotional connections with your characters so that they feel fully lifelike. This allows your audience to truly believe in the story and experience it as if it were real. In order to do this, you must know everything about your character – their strengths, weaknesses and what drives them.

This process involves understanding your character and getting inside their head so that you can imagine what they're thinking, feeling and believing. It also means understanding the non-verbal aspects of their personality – body language and gestures. This will allow you to convey your character's emotions and thoughts through their actions.

While it's important to understand your character's backstory and their personal journey, it's equally essential to understand their current characterization. This is what will give you an idea of their current personality and how they'll react to the dramatic events in the scene.

For example, if your character's strength is talking to strangers and gaining their trust, this might be beneficial in the beginning of the story. However, if this trait is what's driving your character to make certain decisions in the plot, it might become detrimental to the outcome of your story.

It's a good idea to make a list of your character's personality traits and then boil them down to their most essential qualities. This is a quick way to remember them and will help you create a deeper connection with your character. You can even categorize these qualities into positive and negative, as many of them may be both.

As an actor, you're not going to be able to empathize with your characters if you're constantly judging their choices and actions. Therefore, you must set aside your evaluative judgments to try and see things from your character's perspective. This is known as higher-order empathy.

If you're having trouble empathizing with your character, it might be helpful to think about your own experiences and what you would do in their situation. This is a great way to create empathy in your character and develop a more authentic connection with readers.

Why Script Analysis Is Important to Actors and Writers

Whether you are working on a feature film, a short film or a television show, completing a top-to-bottom screenplay is a major accomplishment. It is now time to take the next step and break down your script.

The process is called Script Analysis. It begins with a cold read.

Breakdown

A script breakdown is the process of highlighting and organizing each element of a film's story into an easily accessible and organized production plan. It's a conversion of the script from a story-driven creative document into a practical production guide that can be used to prepare, budget and schedule all aspects of a film's pre-production.

A detailed and thorough breakdown of a script can be the difference between a successful film and one that flounders due to lack of funding, time or talent. Creating a breakdown requires a great deal of attention and detail, and is often a collaborative effort between different departments on a film set. Depending on the project, the breakdown can include elements such as: locations; camera angles; costumes; props; and stage (or set) direction.

The first step in breaking down a script is to read it thoroughly. It's important to read it without judging it and to enjoy the story if possible. Once you've finished reading it, highlight the identifying information for each scene. This can be done with a marker or pencil, and may include stage directions, character names and the actor's lines. It's also helpful to cross out any dialogue that can be omitted from the final film.

After completing this task, you should have an overall understanding of the production requirements for each scene. Using modern script breakdown software, this process is simplified to an easy click-and-drag experience. Once you've imported your script, it automatically categorizes each scene scene by scene. You can then select and tag each element that you want to appear on your breakdown sheet. You can even add your own custom categories if necessary.

After tagging each element, you can transfer all of the highlighted information to its appropriate list on the breakdown summary sheet. Having all of this information neatly organized into an easy-to-read format will help everyone on the production team understand what their individual responsibilities are and where additional resources or time may be needed. Upon completion, the breakdown can be distributed to all relevant departments and crew members.

Character Motivations

During script analysis, it's important to determine character motivation. Understanding why a character says and does things makes them more relatable to the reader. It also helps a writer and actor understand what makes them tick and what might be driving their choices in a scene or overall story arc. For example, if a character throws a fit in their hotel room, it's important to know the reason behind it. It could be a simple thing like being a guest in the wrong place, but it could be something more complex, such as feeling rejected by their S.O. or having unresolved issues from their past.

Identifying these motivations is often done by looking at a character's given circumstances and determining their internal and external conflicts. Using these conflicting factors to create more interesting and complex character motivations can take an otherwise one-dimensional goal and turn it into a compelling story line. For example, a character might have the desire to get revenge on their ex, but if they have a knotty character flaw that is keeping them from getting it, it gives them a greater sense of internal conflict.

Knowing a character's motivation can help a writer figure out how to best achieve their beats and what actions will be most effective in a scene. For example, if a character's primary professional drive is to solve a crime, they might use their internal conflict of having to provide for their family as a way to push them to work harder. This can add depth to their performance and make them more realistic to read.

Many people are familiar with Meisner technique, which uses intensive repetition exercises to bring actors out of their heads and into the moment. However, few people realise that Meisner was also a stickler for script analysis and used many of Stanislavsky's methods. In fact, he had his actors do a number of questions to determine their characters' emotional circumstances in addition to their given circumstances. These questions are similar to those that are suggested in this book and can be incorporated into any script analysis exercise, helping writers to uncover patterns and themes in a dramatic text.

Through-Line

In the world of acting, through-line refers to the overall story arc that propels a character's journey. This is more than just a big plot question your audience will be eager to see answered – it's also a specific theme or idea the playwright wants you to feel at the end of the story. It might be about heroism, family loyalty or even love. In this sense, the through-line is like a golden thread that holds together all the smaller scenes into one cohesive story your audience will enjoy and remember.

The through-line was first suggested by Constantin Stanislavski as a simplified way to help actors understand their characters. He believed that each actor should be aware of their objective in any scene, but

they should also strive to understand the "thread" that linked all these objectives together and pushed their character forward. He called this concept the Super Objective, and it is essentially the through-line of a script.

Once your objectives are clear, you can start to work on determining beats and actions. This is where your textual analysis will really pay off – examining the word choices around verbs, adverbs and adjectives will give you clues about how your character might best achieve their goal in any given scene. In addition, you'll want to keep in mind that a new beat doesn't necessarily call for a new action: sometimes the status quo shifts simply because your character hasn't exhausted the effectiveness of their last choice.

For many people, the process of script analysis is an organic, intuitive experience that grows as they spend time with a piece of writing. However, as the industry continues to evolve, technology is making this process more streamlined and accessible than ever before. Using artificial intelligence to analyze a script, writers, producers and directors can gain valuable insight into the potential of their story by making more informed predictions based on real data. This is a powerful tool that could potentially change the way movies are made in the future. By analyzing a script's genre, characters and dialogue, AI algorithms can make more informed decisions about what type of film will succeed at the box office.

Acting

The acting process is different for each actor, but all good actors analyze their scripts to develop an original and truthful portrayal. The more time and effort that an actor puts into their character, the better they will perform on stage or onset. Analyzing a script helps an actor understand their character's motivations and objectives, which allows them to make strong choices during performance.

The first step in script analysis is to read the entire script from start to finish. This ensures that the actor is familiar with the script and has all the information needed to play their role. It is also helpful to reread the script a few times to refresh your memory of the details.

When analyzing a screenplay, look for patterns of sound, sight and sense. All written works contain these elements, and understanding how they are used can help you to fully embody the text by engaging it intellectually, emotionally and physically. These patterns charge the story, create beats and provide purposeful blocking to support action.

Next, identify all the facts about your character that are included in the given circumstances of each scene. This may include their physical and emotional states, what they do for a living, what type of people are closest to them and any other significant facts about their life. These are the "givens" that drive your objective in each scene, and they will help you to determine what type of actions and emotions are appropriate to pursue.

Lastly, you will want to determine the specific tactics that your character uses in pursuit of their objective in each scene. This will often be tied to a particular beat in the scene, and the way in which you achieve this objective will vary depending on your director's vision and the character's overall objectives. For example, you may choose to use bound movements to imply that your character is on guard, while someone else might use more fluid and free-floating movement to imply openness and a willingness to experience new things.

This process of breaking down a script can be done on your own or with the guidance of a professional. Many theatre schools have programs that can help you learn to analyze a script and prepare for a role.

Request more information about a bachelor's degree in theatre from us today!

The Power of Improvisation

When most people hear the word "improv," they think of a group of comedians performing in front of an audience. However, improvisation also has a powerful impact in other areas.

Improvisation involves collaboration, creativity and being responsive to one another - skills that can be applied in many areas of life. The Power of Improvisation focuses on the following key principles:

Spontaneity

The ability to be spontaneous is a valuable skill for many reasons, from fostering creativity to reducing stress. However, it can be difficult to balance spontaneity with planning in everyday life. Fortunately, understanding the difference between the two can help you improve your spontaneity in the workplace and beyond.

When it comes to improvisation, being spontaneous requires a willingness to take risks and be flexible in real time. For example, if you are improvising with another actor on stage, it's important to listen closely to what they're saying and follow their lead, even if you don't agree. It's also important to be open to unexpected opportunities, as they may arise when you least expect them.

The ability to improvise is an essential part of creativity, as it allows you to think on your feet and react in the moment. While improvisation is often associated with creative arts such as comedy or music, it can also be used in the workplace to boost productivity and teamwork.

In a recent study, researchers found that incorporating improvisation into spontaneous speech practice in foreign language teaching increased student teachers' confidence in speaking spontaneously in class. The researchers believe that using improv methodology during spontaneous speech practice in EFL teacher education could have a positive impact on the development of student teachers' fluency and their professional identity as teachers.

Participants were exposed to improvisation exercises in small groups. This reduced their prior negative associations with spontaneous speech practice and enabled them to explore the fictional world of the improv games while feeling safe and supported by their peers. This collaborative improvisation approach was particularly beneficial for reluctant speakers, who were more comfortable with this type of learning experience in smaller groups than in larger groups. In addition, the humour of the improvisation exercises reduced their anxiety.

Ultimately, being spontaneous is all about embracing risk and enjoying the freedom that spontaneity can provide. So next time you have a meeting, instead of checking your day planner, try ditching the plan and say "Yes, and..." to the unexpected opportunity.

Creativity

Improvisation is a tool that can be taken from the stage and used to achieve better business outcomes offstage in fast-paced, dynamic environments. It aids in creativity and collaboration, both essential skills for innovation. It helps people to think on their feet, work outside the prescribed path and explore creative solutions that have never been thought of before.

In a time when companies must be flexible and quick to adapt to changing circumstances, the skills learned in improv can help managers and employees lead their teams through challenges and paradigm shifts with greater ease. It's also important for individuals to be able to think quickly on their feet in everyday situations like meeting new people, navigating through traffic jams or having an unexpected conversation with a friend.

The "yes, and" mentality of improvisation encourages participants to build upon the ideas of their scene partners rather than trying to be right all the time. It allows participants to develop a deeper understanding of their colleagues' perspectives and to create a collaborative mindset that is critical in the workplace.

Improvisation also teaches individuals to trust themselves and their instincts. This is a crucial skill for anyone to have, especially in a career where the ability to make quick decisions can be a survival factor. Moreover, improv teaches participants to let go of the fear of looking stupid or getting it wrong, which is the biggest obstacle for many people in taking risks at work.

Practicing improv in a safe and fun environment is the best way to learn these skills. With the support of an experienced teacher, a person is able to practice and self-reflect on their learnings in an experiential, non-judgmental setting. This leads to a personal growth that is transferable to all aspects of a person's life, including their professional lives and relationships.

Developing improvisational skills is essential for any business leader, regardless of industry. Whether they're dealing with new regulatory requirements or navigating the Covid-19 pandemic, managers and employees who have the flexibility to think on their feet can navigate unpredictable and complex scenarios with success. This is why leadership training programs should include improvisational exercises as part of their curriculum.

Collaboration

Improvisation can help to foster collaboration among team members. It is a great way to build trust and develop communication skills. It also helps to develop creative ideas. For example, improv can be used in dance to create unique choreographies. It teaches dancers to be bold and follow their instincts. It also teaches them to be flexible and accept failure. This can be an important lesson for business, as companies often face setbacks and need to be able to adapt quickly.

Improvization also aids in spontaneity, which is a crucial element of creativity. Being spontaneous is not easy, but it can be a great way to make art. Artists like Oliver Herring and Abraham Cruzvillegas use improvisation in their work to develop new ideas and create unexpected outcomes.

The spontaneity of improvisation enables artists to create something fresh and exciting every time they perform. It is a technique that many performers use in their work to inspire themselves and create more creative and interesting performances. Improvisation is a great tool for aspiring artists who want to break free from the constraints of traditional art forms.

Unlike other forms of theatre, improvisation relies on the support of others to succeed. It requires the cooperation of all participants to create a performance that is enjoyable for the audience. The improvisers must be aware of one another's choices and react expressively together. They must also work together to maintain a balance of freedom and constraints. This can be a difficult balance to achieve in the workplace, but it is necessary for success.

Improvisation is a form of collaborative creativity that can be used to enhance a person's sense of well-being. Research shows that it can help to develop the social component of eudaimonia, as defined by

Seligman's PERMA model of well-being. In addition, it can be used to promote a positive attitude towards oneself and to develop social bonds with other people.

In order to become a good improviser, it is essential to learn the rules of the game. One such rule is the 'yes and' principle, which means that the performers must agree with everything their scene partner says and then build upon it. For example, if your scene partner says that you are on a spaceship, you must accept it and then add to it with your own ideas about the situation. This teaches the performers to be open to the ideas of their colleagues and to be flexible in their thinking.

Active Listening

One of the most fundamental aspects of improvisation is active listening. The ability to listen and respond in the moment is a skill that can be applied to both personal and professional settings. The old adage of practice makes perfect holds true for this skill and the more often people engage in improv the better they become at it.

During a scene in improv, actors are encouraged to "read their environment" and listen for key words to jump start their next response. This skill helps them to be present and engaged with their scene partners, which is crucial for creating an effective collaborative performance.

It also aids in spontaneity and creativity. When someone is thinking about what they will say next, they are not fully engaging with the current situation. This is a common trap that many people fall into when discussing business issues with their peers. It can be difficult to break out of this cycle of reverting back to the familiar "No, but..." mindset.

The other benefit of improv is its ability to develop empathy. As people become more proficient in improv, they are taught to put themselves in other people's shoes and react to their actions as if it were happening to them. This can be a valuable skill in the business world, as it allows you to better understand the perspectives of others and see things from their point of view.

In addition, improv encourages individuals to take risks and step outside of their comfort zone. This can be a great way to build confidence and learn how to operate outside of your comfort zone, which will help you in the business world when you are interacting with clients or colleagues.

The skills learned in improv are not just useful for the acting world, but are essential for all of life. By allowing participants to experience learning on an intellectual, physical and emotional level, improv provides the framework for personal growth that can be applied in all areas of a person's life. The benefits of improv are far reaching and it is important for businesses to offer these opportunities to their employees as a way to improve the quality of interactions at work and beyond.

The Rehearsal Process

Whether you are in a jazz band or a rock group, rehearsals assemble the pieces of your performance. They catch mistakes in practiced details and help musicians develop the chemistry and great practiced skill level audiences want to see and hear at live shows and on records.

The technical rehearsal is where you walk through the entire show in performance order. It involves making sure every light cue, music cue and microphone works as planned.

Rehearsal Room Dynamics

Rehearsals can be labor intensive and require a lot of work from everyone involved. However, a great rehearsal is an opportunity for everyone to get excited about the show and to feel like they have accomplished something together. If everyone is excited about the show, it can help the actors to perform better. In addition, a good rehearsal will also help the crew members to perform their jobs more efficiently.

During the rehearsal process, it is important to keep all the actors focused on what they need to do in order to make the scene work. This can be done by limiting distractions as much as possible. In addition, it is important to keep the actors engaged with each other through the use of improvisational exercises. These exercises can help the actors to find new ways to approach the scene and can unlock the potential of the scene.

Rehearsal rooms should be equipped with the necessary equipment to isolate sound, such as an acoustic ceiling or floating floor. Acoustic isolation is particularly important in small rehearsal studios, where the walls can be thin and prone to sound leakage. This can be overcome by using an acoustic ceiling or by installing a floating floor made of neoprene or compressed glass fiber.

In larger rehearsal studios, it is a good idea to install a mixing console to allow the musicians to hear each other clearly and adjust their sounds accordingly. In addition, a good rehearsal room should have the appropriate number of microphones to cover all the musicians in the band and allow them to hear themselves at all times.

Many rehearsal facilities are now incorporating recording studios into their facilities, a trend that has been fueled by the boom in live music. Kent Nielsen, who runs Fort Knox, one of the largest rehearsal facilities in the country, believes that these studios will continue to grow and expand as touring artists increasingly demand a range of services from their rehearsal studios. This may include acoustic isolation, recording equipment and a lounge space for post-rehearsal discussion.

Scenes

The first period of rehearsal is typically devoted to prioritizing a unity of understanding of the story itself. This can take a week or more to get everyone on the same page, but it is essential. Without this common artistic ground, the rest of the process can quickly become confused and chaotic.

Once this has been achieved, the director and actors can begin shaping the scenes of the production. The actor's job is to identify the scene questions within each scene and answer them. These questions may be introduced at the beginning, end or even partway through a scene. The answers will then be shaped so they lead on the path to the overarching story question. The director will also ensure that each scene has a strong physical life and that the blocking is clear.

By the time of the dress rehearsal, which is usually at the end of technical week, the entire production should be fairly well shaped. However, there may still be some issues that need to be ironed out. This is the point at which the producer should start promoting the play to the public. This can be done through fliers, school announcements, newspaper coverage and other advertising methods.

During this phase of the rehearsal, it is also important to have a good balance between group and individual work. Group work allows each actor to receive feedback from other members of the ensemble, which is crucial for the creative development of the performance. Individual work, on the other hand, can be an opportunity for each actor to develop their unique interpretation of the character they are playing.

It is at this point that it becomes a good idea for the cast to start working "off book" (without their scripts). Unless they are confident that they have memorized their lines, it can be helpful for the director or stage manager to be on hand to "throw lines" to the actors when needed. This should always be done in a supportive and nonjudgmental manner. The actors should be encouraged to conserve their voices, as they will likely need to speak for hours at this point in the rehearsal.

Collaboration Between Actors & Directors

In rehearsals, the director is able to establish a relationship with actors and create an environment that allows them to take risks and explore their characters. They must provide clear communication of their vision for the character and scene while remaining open to feedback.

In addition to working with their actors, directors must also work with the rest of the production staff to ensure that they are capturing the desired look and feel of the show. They may hold production meetings where they discuss all the elements that will come together to make a finished product such as lighting, set design and costumes.

Rehearsal schedules vary depending on the type of show being rehearsed. For example, a two-person play or art song might be rehearsed only with the two actors present; a theatre performance with only actors may be rehearsed with just the stage manager and director in attendance. On the other hand, a musical or acrobatic-focused circus might be rehearsed with the full cast and crew present.

Once all the actor-specific work has been completed, it is time to begin blocking scenes and rehearsaling with props and sets. The director must be able to balance the need to block everything with keeping the process fresh and exciting for the actors.

As the actors continue to delve into their characters and build the imaginary world of the show, they will likely be asked by the director to make more and more choices for their performances. These choices must fit within the world being built by the ensemble, and must correspond with the other acting choices that are happening across the ensemble.

The last few days of rehearsal are the longest for the company. It is at this point that the director's capacity for patience and self-control are put to the test. At this point the ensemble has been rehearsing for weeks and is probably very close to what will be a finished product. Scenes are rehearsed on the actual set and lighting cues need to be established.

During this time, it is not unusual for the cast to be tired and grumpy. They have spent weeks rehearsing in the same space, often on their own after a long day of running through the show with the designers.

Technical Rehearsals

The technical rehearsals are the part of the rehearsal process when all the different elements of the production come together to create a finished product. This includes lighting, sound, costumes, scenery, props and even special effects such as fog or haze.

These rehearsals are usually held in the space where the performance will be taking place. The tech rehearsals can take a long time to complete because they often involve running through the entire show multiple times to make sure that all the technology is working properly and is in sync with all other elements of the production.

During the tech rehearsals, it is important that the actors are allowed to explore the set and learn where all the props and equipment are located. This will allow them to become familiar with the physicality of the set and also allows them to get a feel for how they are going to move around in the set. It is also at this point that the stage manager should explain to the actors all the administrative matters such as the rehearsal schedule, contact list, and shop hour requirements.

This is also the time when prop tracking should be done. This involves creating a clear sheet that will let the actors know where all their props are and how they go to and from them. This will save time during the rehearsal process when actors are constantly asking their assistant stage managers where their 50,000 props are hidden in backstage.

It is also a good time to test all the necessary technology for the show such as projectors, screens, computer programs and the sound system. This will help avoid any issues that may arise on the day of the production.

If the tech rehearsals are running long and affecting the actor's ability to perform in other activities, it is the stage manager's job to politely notify the director. While some directors are okay with continuing on, it is a good idea to give them the option to stop the rehearsal if needed. This way the actors don't lose out on an opportunity that they had planned for.

Voice and Diction

Good diction is NOT about changing your accent or making you "talk posh". It's about clarity.

Inflection conveys mood to an audience – irony, sarcasm and jokes are examples. This is also where the "tone" of your speech comes into play. Tone is everything from excitement to monotone. It affects articulation, clarity and even the way you pronounce certain words.

Techniques for voice modulation

Voice modulation is an important skill for public speaking, and can help you create a powerful impact on your audience. You can use different techniques to make your voice sound more dynamic, including adjusting your pitch and tone, adding pauses, and stressing certain words. While it may seem difficult to master, learning how to do this can help you keep your audience's attention throughout your speech. The best way to learn these techniques is to practice with a friend or family member who can provide honest feedback about your performance.

Using the right modulation techniques can make your voice sound more natural and confident. You can also improve the clarity of your speech by slowing down your speed, choosing the right words, and emphasizing the key points of your presentation. This will allow you to convey a sense of authority and professionalism to your audience. You can even use inflection to add emotion and authenticity to your speech, although you should avoid monotone as this can be very boring to listen to.

To improve the clarity of your voice, try to pronounce every word clearly and enunciate each syllable. This will ensure that your audience can understand what you are saying, and will be able to follow your presentation easily. In addition, it is important to avoid mumbling and swallowing your words. This will lead to a difficult to understand accent and can cause your audience to lose interest in your speech.

Another useful technique for improving your voice is to practice humming or singing exercises to strengthen the muscles of your vocal cords. You can find many free humming and singing lessons online, as well as tutorials by voice coaches and experts. However, it is important to remember that these techniques should be used sparingly as too much pressure can strain the vocal cords and cause discomfort.

You can also learn about voice culture, which is the methodology used to train a person's voice to sing effectively. This is a popular and widely accepted method of voice training, and many people have found it to be beneficial in enhancing their vocal range and quality. While some critics claim that voice culture can be unnatural and forceful, others say it can be a useful tool for overcoming speech impediments like stuttering. The Bridge Technique is a good example of voice culture, and it has been shown to be effective in improving the voice of many public speakers. It is also helpful in reducing the risk of vocal injury.

Clarity of speech

Having clarity of speech is very important, especially in business. A clear speaker is more confident and can make a stronger impact on the listener. Clarity of speech also means using proper articulation, word choice and inflection to communicate emotion. While many people think of diction as the art of pronunciation, it is more than just that. In the world of acting and singing, diction describes the overall expressiveness of words in terms of articulation, word choice and inflection.

Practicing speech exercises is one of the best ways to improve your clarity of voice. Try to speak slowly and pronounce each syllable carefully. This can help you avoid getting tired while speaking. Another great way to improve your clarity of speech is to practice breathing exercises. You can do this by holding your breath for a short time and then exhaling slowly. It will increase your oxygen levels and reduce the stress on your vocal cords.

It is also helpful to use specific numbers, instead of vague words like "many" or "some." Using concrete, specific language will ensure that your audience understands what you are saying. In addition, you should also avoid slang, jargon and vague pop-culture references. You can also strengthen your speech clarity by practicing jaw exercises. Open your mouth wide and hum gently to stretch the muscles in your face and jaw. Repeat this exercise several times, and then close your mouth to re-tune the muscle.

Improving the clarity of your speech can be difficult. Some techniques to try include avoiding jumping around thoughts, finishing sentences properly, expanding vocabulary, removing unnecessary information, communicating one thought at a time and pausing before speaking. These tips will help you improve your clarity of speech and establish credibility at work and in personal relationships.

Analyzing and emulating eloquent speakers is another great way to improve your clarity of speech. This will give you the confidence to express your ideas clearly. It will also enable you to articulate your thoughts without the use of filler words like "um" or "like".

You can also improve your speech clarity by learning to be more organized and preparing for speeches. This will prevent you from rambling and sounding unprepared. It is also important to be able to identify the main points of your speech before you begin.

You can teach your students the importance of diction by having them read passages of text and identify how the author's word choice contributes to the tone and mood of the text. You can then ask them to rewrite the passage using different words with contrasting connotations. They can then compare the two passages to see how their diction has changed the tone and mood of the text.

Accent work

An accent is a way of speaking that can influence the meaning and pronunciation of words. It can also influence the rhythm and phrasing of a speech. For example, if you speak with an accent that is slurred or nasal, it can have a negative impact on the meaning of your speech. Using an accent can also make it difficult for others to understand you, which can affect your social interactions.

An accent can be a result of genetics, upbringing, or environment. It can also be caused by learning a new language. When learning a foreign language, an accent can occur when the speaker substitutes sounds from their native language with similar sounds from the language they are trying to learn. This can cause them to sound foreign or "strange."

It is important to know how to recognize and improve your accents, especially if you are an actor. There are several exercises that can help you improve your diction and accents. One is to listen to public speakers, such as politicians and celebrities, and attempt to imitate their articulation. Another is to practice your articulation by saying tongue twisters and chants. This helps to train the mouth muscles and slows down thought so that you can pronounce each word clearly.

Dialect is often confused with accent, but they are different things. Accents are the differences in a person's pronunciation, intonation, and sound features, while dialect is the overall style of a spoken language.

Generally, dialect is closer to the first definition, while accent is more of an embellishment.

The best way to improve your diction is to practice regularly. You should not only work on articulation exercises before reading text, but also throughout your day. This will ensure that your articulation is clear and consistent. It is also a good idea to listen to people who have great diction to get an idea of what it should look like.

You can also try listening to recordings of different accents and practicing them. However, you should avoid relying on stereotypical representations of accents. These stereotypes can be offensive to the speakers and make them feel less valued. Moreover, if you try to do a character's accent based on a stereotype, you will not be able to master the technical aspects of that accent. You should focus on learning the phonetics of the accent before you create a character.

In general, Sammi recommends training for a standard British accent, or RP. This is a common accent that most voice actors do. She prefers this accent over other regional accents because it is more flexible and allows the actor to express themselves through a wide range of characters. It is also the most popular choice for voice overs.

Physicality and Movement

A healthy amount of physical activity helps prevent disease and reduces the risk of premature death. People of all ages should do at least 150 minutes of moderate-intensity exercise or 75 minutes of vigorous-intensity exercise each week.

It is becoming increasingly accepted that movement is more than just about weight loss and improving physical appearance. It also contributes to overall mental health and wellbeing.

Body Language

Body language is communication conveyed through movement and position, particularly facial expressions and gestures. This type of non-verbal communication is often added to the words spoken and can be very important in understanding the full message being conveyed. The way that people communicate with body language can vary by age, gender and social situation. Body language can also be influenced by the culture of the person and therefore must be carefully analysed.

Facial expressions, such as smiles, frowns, eyebrow raising and eye rolls are one example of body language. Gestures, such as waving and pointing, are another. Posture, including slouching, leaning in or crossing arms can also indicate a range of emotions. Eye contact and avoiding eye contact are other examples of body language. Touch can also be a form of body language, with handshakes, pats on the back and hugs all having different meanings. Body language can also give away health information, with certain movements indicating disease.

Learning to read and interpret body language can be a crucial tool for any actor. It can help them to understand the intention behind the words that are being spoken and allow them to make adjustments to their own body language to support the scene. This can be particularly useful when working with a script that relies heavily on dialogue, as it can often be difficult to tell the audience what a character is feeling through their voice alone.

Understanding the importance of body language can be further enhanced by studying the work of acting greats and familiarising yourself with movement techniques like Laban Movement Analysis and Viewpoints. It can be used by actors to communicate a vast range of emotions and to add depth and authenticity to a performance. This can be especially beneficial when working with a script that requires them to portray characters from different social backgrounds or cultures. It can also be helpful when working with a script that relies on physical theatre and/or pantomime. This is where the true magic happens, when the right combinations of body language and recognised facial expressions are used to create powerful performances.

Stage Combat

Stage combat is the specialized language actors use to keep themselves safe and create spectacular fight choreography that wows audiences. It requires precise technique and attention to detail, but it also teaches students how to connect with their fellow performers onstage through their shared passion for the physicality of the work.

The basic elements of stage combat are striking and blocking, a process that allows an actor to demonstrate a character's emotions through their movement and actions. Practicing and mastering these skills helps an actor develop their ability to take risks onstage, which is important in creating realistic emotional connections with their audience.

In addition to being an integral part of the acting experience, learning stage combat can help improve an actor's overall physical fitness. Aside from providing a great cardio workout, the exercises involved in stage combat are an excellent way to build balance, strength and endurance. In addition, the discipline of learning and practicing the choreography helps an actor develop their focus and concentration.

Fights in plays, musicals and film present a character's most primal, emotionally heightened state. They depict rage, fear, aggression and anxiety, all of which are very real human feelings. This makes them challenging for the audience to watch.

As a result, most professional productions that contain onstage violence hire a fight director to choreograph the fighting and elect a fight captain to ensure the safety of the cast over the run of the show. While it is not impossible for an untrained actor to successfully perform a violent scene, it is extremely risky for the actors involved and can quickly derail the story.

Dr Grant recounts an anecdote in which an actor she worked with refused to follow her advice, insisting on using stage combat techniques even though the script called for a simple slap. She believes that this shows a lack of understanding or appreciation for the skill and craft required to safely execute a complicated fight sequence onstage.

A well-choreographed fight sequence includes both offensive and defensive actions, as well as a variety of other movements to convey emotion and intensity. Actors must be able to react convincingly to their partner's moves so that the audience can suspend disbelief and believe that each strike was delivered in a real and visceral manner.

In addition to coordinating physical action, a good fight sequence is accompanied by the right sound effects. A groan, gasp or grunt from the actor can be as convincing as a physical blow for an audience when it is timed precisely to the moment of impact.

Stage combat training can also teach an actor how to safely and effectively interact with other performers in a physically demanding situation. It can help them understand when a scene is unsafe and how to advocate for themselves, so they are not asked to risk injury.

Dance

Dance is a form of physical expression that encompasses a wide range of movements. It can be used to tell a story, communicate emotion, and convey meaning. It can also be used to create a specific mood or atmosphere in a performance. In addition to conveying an emotional message, dance can also be used as a means of recreation or socializing.

Incorporating dance and other forms of movement into your acting can help you to develop a more expressive and three-dimensional character. It can also help you to use your body in ways that are more natural and engaging for an audience. Incorporating movement into your acting can also help you to overcome any bad habits that might be inhibiting your ability to perform. Incorporating movement into your acting work is especially important if you have a background in dancing, as it can be difficult for dancers to translate their skills into the acting world.

There are many different types of dance, with the most common being theatrical dance. Dramatic dance is intended to express character, emotion, and narrative action through the use of specific movements. Other types of dance include folk and ceremonial dance, which may be used for a variety of reasons, including celebrating an event or occasion, hunting and courtship dances, and pantomimic gestures that are used to communicate a particular mood or idea.

The most important aspect of dance is the energy that is conveyed through the movement. This can be communicated through a number of different aspects, including attack, shape, space, and time. Attack refers to the speed and intensity of the movement. Shape refers to the way the movement takes on a certain shape, such as circular or straight. Space refers to the area in which the movement is taking place. Time refers to the duration of the movement in terms of seconds, minutes, or hours.

For example, a dancer might utilize a sharp, percussive attack, have a choppy flow of movement that is interrupted by pauses, or have a lot of directional changes in their steps. The amount of weight the dancer uses can also communicate a specific feeling, such as heaviness or gravity, or lightness and upward movement. The overall quality of the movement is also important, such as being tight and structured or smooth and flowing.

While some actors may argue that dance and acting are two different art forms, there are some similarities between the two. Both require a certain level of physical movement and both involve using the body to convey emotions and ideas. In addition, both acting and dance often incorporate music in their work. For instance, the floating gondola waltz in PHANTOM and the staccato strut of the soldiers in SAIGON are examples of dancing in musical theatre.

The Emotional Life of an Actor

Emotional work must not jeopardize the actor's mental sanity and should only be used as preparation. Sanford Meisner emphasized this and taught that actors must create imaginary circumstances and an emotional life for their characters.

This requires rehearsal and eventually transforms into performance. An actor's higher-order empathic understanding of her character can fold into this embodied experience. This is known as double attunement.

Understanding and portraying complex emotions

As an actor, it is critical to develop empathy for the people you play and the people around them. The more you understand the emotional nuances of relationships, the more powerful and believable your performances will be.

This is a key element to developing complex emotions, and it requires an understanding of the Four Pillars of Acting: Empathy, Physicality, Presence and Emotional Life. When you work on this aspect of acting, it can take an emotional toll, but the results are well worth it.

One mistake that many actors make is to think that they must feel all of the emotions their characters are feeling in order to be able to portray them convincingly. This is a common misconception and a dangerous way to approach acting. If you are trying to force yourself to feel the emotions your character is having, it will be obvious to the audience and will make them less engaged with your performance.

The best way to understand and portray complicated emotions is by using imagination and focusing on the process of building the character. This will allow you to create a sense of empathy for the other characters in the scene and help you find the right emotions to portray. Using your imagination can also be useful when it comes to exploring emotional scenarios that you have not personally experienced, but need to be able to express effectively on stage.

When performing, it is important to remember that the audience is looking for a genuine and realistic experience. This is especially true when it comes to emotionally traumatic scenes. Actors need to be able to connect with the audience and transport them into the scene so that they can feel what the character is feeling. This is not easy, but it can be done if the actor takes the time to prepare for the scene by imagining their own experiences and allowing themselves to feel the emotions that would accompany them.

In acting class, there are a lot of instructors who will make a big deal about working an actor up to the point that they begin to cry. While this can be an effective technique for some actors, it is important to remember that once you are onstage, you are no longer the actor who is trying to get the audience to cry – you are the character and must focus solely on giving a performance that will resonate with the audience.

A great way to practice preparing for a difficult scene is by practicing specificization, a process developed by Sanford Meisner. This involves programming authentic feelings into a particular circumstance of the character. This can be difficult, as the actor may need to imagine and experience difficult emotions that are not currently present in their lives. However, by establishing healthy boundaries with regard to emotional preparation and knowing what is acceptable resistance, the actor can overcome this obstacle.

The psychological toll and rewards of deep emotional work

In the world of acting, there is a lot of work that goes into emotionally connecting to your character. Some of that work involves evoking difficult emotions, such as anger, fear, or sadness. For many people, these types of feelings are very hard to experience in a natural and healthy way. Fortunately, there are ways to help. During the training process, actors are often taught techniques to help them overcome these barriers. This type of emotional work is known as deep acting.

Using techniques such as breathing, body movement, and putting yourself in the shoes of your character can help you access more complex emotions. However, it takes a great deal of time and energy to break down these barriers. In addition, the emotional toll can sometimes be high, and this can lead to stress, anxiety, and depression. For this reason, it's important for actors to take good care of themselves during the process of deep acting.

One of the biggest challenges is determining how much to "show" and how much to hold back. Many actors will start by trying to "show" all their emotions. This can make the performance more realistic, but it can also be extremely difficult for an actor to maintain. In addition, it can be challenging to know when to hold back and when to let go.

Some actors will also struggle with the fact that they may not experience the same feelings as their characters. This is an important point to keep in mind, especially if you're working in the world of commercial acting, where the lines between the personal and professional lives can be blurred.

It's also important to remember that the emotional toll of deep acting is not necessarily permanent. In addition, overcoming emotional barriers can be very rewarding. It's important to be careful not to push too far too fast, however, because you can easily become mentally exhausted.

There are some classes that seem to make a big deal about "working an actor up" to the point of crying. This can include asking invasive questions that are better suited for a qualified therapist, such as questions about rape, incest, and physical and sexual abuse. These types of questions are inappropriate for an acting class, and they can be psychologically harmful.

In the world of customer service, displaying positive emotions is a consistent mantra for front-line team members. This has led to some workers experiencing emotional exhaustion, which can lead to poor job satisfaction, lower work engagement and even emotional disorders (Humphrey et al., 2015). Fortunately, researchers have found that deep acting can reduce this effect. In fact, this type of emotion display appears to be superior to surface acting in terms of the effect it has on worker well-being and performance.

Experiencing difficult emotions

Emotional life requires a lot of courage, stamina and creativity from actors. Whether you are working on a scene, an audition or a full performance, emotional work is never something that can be played or pushed, but rather a process of transforming the character's meanings into your own authentically. It is an emotional journey that is always a bit of a maze, and one that takes a great deal of time to master.

The most important step is understanding what your emotions are trying to tell you. Difficult emotions, like anger, jealousy and fear, are trying to alert you that something is wrong in your life. They are not personal attacks on you, but rather signals that a situation needs your attention and care.

Once you understand what your difficult emotions are trying to tell you, they will no longer have control over you and can be harnessed for acting purposes. You may need to practice the technique of separating yourself from your emotion so that you can observe it objectively. A good way to do this is through meditation, exercise or a simple activity, such as writing. You can also try to be the observer while your emotions pass through you, allowing them to move through your body and mind without controlling you.

A common technique used by actor's is called emotional memory, which involves reliving a specific experience from your own life to invoke the particular feeling required for a scene or moment. This idea was popularized by Constantin Stanislavski, and later by his student Lee Strasberg, who developed The American Method. While this approach can be effective, it often results in a disconnect between the actor and the character and ignores the power of relationship as an essential aspect of drama.

As an alternative to emotional memory, you can practice daydreaming, or letting your imagination play with your feelings. Just be sure to stick with the core four emotions (happiness, sadness, anger and fear) and do not try to work on envy or pride or insecurity, for example. The important thing is to be ruthless in dismantling the blocks that prevent you from being fully accessible to feeling, because these blocks are often subconscious and rooted in myths passed down through generations, telling us that emotion is not productive, masculine, strong or appropriate.

Ultimately, excellent actors are those who feel what they are portraying, and can summon those feelings at will, whether for a few take on a film set or night after night in the theatre. This is a tremendous amount of emotional endurance and strength, and it is a credit to the performers that they have the ability to do so, as well as the dedication and training that gets them there.

Audition Techniques - Choosing the Right Monologue

A strong sense of stage presence and acting is critical for any audition. Choosing character movements that send cooperative cues to your audience illustrates good technique.

During an audition, a director may ask the actor to change something about their performance. This is usually because they want to see a different approach or because of time constraints.

Monologue Selection

A monologue is a great way for actors to show off their acting ability and range. However, choosing the right monologue can be difficult. There are many options out there, and it is important to find a monologue that matches your casting type and captures a range of emotions. Additionally, it is important to remember that you will only have four minutes to perform your monologue before the timer rings. This is why it is important to practice your monologues and be prepared for any changes in the script.

A good place to start when searching for a monologue is in your own acting book. Look through your book and choose a few monologues that capture a range of emotions, such as anger, sadness, and happiness. Then read the monologues aloud to see how well they fit your natural speech pattern. Once you have narrowed down your options, pick four monologues that you feel would be a good fit for you.

Another way to find a monologue is to research contemporary playwrights and actors. Doing this can help you discover new monologues that are not in your acting books. It is also a good idea to research directors to find out what types of roles they like to cast.

This can lead to new monologue ideas for auditions that you are considering.

Once you have a few monologues that you are interested in, it is important to practice them before your audition. Practicing your monologues will help you become more comfortable with them and make it easier to memorize them. Practicing will also allow you to work out any problems with the timing of your lines. The more you work on your monologue, the better chance you will have of selecting the perfect one for your audition.

When you are in an audition, it is important to stay present and focus on the audience. This will help you keep your nerves in check and allow you to give a strong performance. You will also want to avoid looking around the room, as this can be distracting to the casting director. This will also make it harder for the casting director to evaluate your performance.

Lastly, it is important to match the monologue you choose to the role you are auditioning for. This will improve your chances of getting the role because the casting director will be able to picture you in that role. Ultimately, the goal is to impress the casting director so they will be more likely to put you in the next round of the process.

By following these tips, you can be more confident in your monologue selection for your next audition. Just remember that it is important to have confidence and believe in yourself. If you do these things, you can be sure that your monologue will impress the casting director and improve your chances of landing the role.

Cold Reading

Often times actors get their sides (scripts/scenes) to an audition just before they are scheduled to start. This is known as a cold reading audition and it is important to be prepared for these types of auditions. The good news is that with some basic tips and practice you can make a successful impression during a cold read.

The main thing is to not worry about memorizing the lines right away. This can be very stressful and it is not necessary in order to perform well. Rather focus on being able to connect with the other characters in the scene, the emotions they are feeling and how your actions can influence theirs. If you have enough time to prepare then it is a good idea to try and get the first couple of lines down and be able to repeat them off the top of your head. This will help you feel confident and relaxed when you are performing your lines.

It is also a good idea to have a copy of the script with you in case you need to reference it. This can help if you aren't quite sure how to pronounce certain words or need to look up a word in a dictionary. It is also a great idea to practice reading out loud as much as possible in your spare time so that you can become familiar with the way the script looks and flows. This will help you when it comes time to do your cold readings in the studio because it will feel more natural and less like a script you are trying to read off of a page.

Another important tip when doing a cold read is to make sure you aren't looking down at your script while your scene partner is speaking. This can be very distracting to the casting director and it will also take you out of character. Instead, hold your side up to chest level and use your thumbs to keep track of where you are in the text. This is a tried and true expert tip for keeping your place and it will ensure you don't have to constantly look down at the script.

When you are doing your lines during the audition, don't be afraid to be physical if the script calls for it. Producers want to see that you can express the emotion of the scene with your body as well as with your voice. This shows your creativity and flexibility as an actor and can be the difference between getting the job and not.

If you have the opportunity, try shooting some video of yourself doing your cold reads. This will give you the chance to see how your mechanics are working and to fix any bad habits. Some of the most common mistakes that actors make when doing a cold read are burying their heads in the script, waving it around, shaking the script (nervousness), rushing, rocking back and forth and holding the script either too high or to one side.

Callbacks

If you are lucky enough to make it to a callback, you should do your best to be as prepared as possible. This is the one chance you get to leave a positive impression on casting directors and show that you are serious about your craft. This is a great time to practice your monologue and ask for feedback from the judges about how you could improve and strengthen it.

If there is a script for the play you are auditioning for, purchase or borrow a copy and read it in advance. It is often the case that actors are asked to read "sides" which are small, hand-picked portions of a full script and so it's important to be familiar with the entire piece. It is also a good idea to watch a film version of the play in order to see how it has been interpreted by other performers, but don't mimic what you've seen; this will not help you stand out from the crowd.

Show up early for your audition. Arriving ten minutes before the audition starts is a good way to show that you are punctual and ready to work. It will also give you a chance to settle in and be alone with your thoughts before entering the audition space.

Be polite and courteous to the people you meet during your audition. The people working on casting are just like you and they all have busy lives that include traffic delays, work pressures, family responsibilities, etc. They will not be impressed if you use the interview portion of your audition to complain about these problems. Be positive, cheerful and friendly and don't talk about your problems during the audition.

When the judges start their interviews, be ready to answer questions and keep them short and to the point. This will help keep the audition moving along in a timely manner and it will also allow you to stay calm and confident. It is a good idea to dress appropriately for the type of role you are trying out for (no jeans, please). If you are auditioning for musical theater, bring a song that relates to the piece and which you know well and enjoy singing.

Be sure to thank the judges for their time at the end of your audition. It is a very simple and effective way to leave a good impression on them and it will make them more likely to remember you as a friendly, courteous person who was very easy to work with. This is especially important if you are competing with other people for the same role, since they will have only limited time to evaluate all of the auditioners that day. This tip is also very important if you do not book the role, as it will leave a positive impression of your gratitude and kindness.

How Acting for the Camera Differs From Stage Acting

Actors who come from a theatre background are often shocked by how much acting for the camera differs. While actors in theatre get weeks to craft a performance, on screen everything is discovered on set and often without the sanctity of rehearsal.

The camera picks up every subtle movement, twitch and even the faintest change in breath. It takes a fine balance of raw honesty and some trickery, magic and cheating to create great cinema.

Stage and Screen Acting

Stage acting and screen acting are two very different disciplines that require a very specific skill set. Although there are many similarities, such as delivering dialogue and conveying emotion, there are also some key differences between the two. One of the most significant differences is in the way that actors must approach their performances. Screen actors must be aware of the camera's perspective and work closely with the director and cinematographer to ensure that their performances are framed effectively. This includes understanding the importance of eye lines and marks. Eye lines refer to the direction an actor looks in relation to the camera while marks are specific positions on the set that the actor must be in at the correct time to capture the shot.

When working on a film set, the actor will often only have a short amount of time to complete their scene. This means that they must be able to work fast and accurately. This can be especially challenging when working with a director who is pushing for a particular look or performance from the actor.

In addition to this, screen acting requires a great deal of preparation ahead of shooting day. The actors must know their script and be able to quickly and accurately read through the scene several times before they arrive on set. They must also be familiar with the lighting and sound requirements of the scene so that they can work with the crew to achieve the desired results.

Another difference between stage and screen acting is that the physical action of a scene must be 'blocked' by the director. This means that the actors will need to practice their blocking until they are able to travel around the set at the right times and be in the correct place for each shot. This is particularly important for screen acting as the camera may be trained in on specific locations, or very tight 'close up' shots, that would be impossible to capture on stage.

Finally, it is important for screen actors to remember that the audience will not be able to turn up the volume on their performance like they can in the theatre. This means that the actors must be loud enough so that they can be heard in the back rows of the audience.

Hitting Marks

One of the biggest differences between stage and camera acting is that on-camera work is more collaborative. The actor needs to work closely with the director and other crew members during filming, which can be a little nerve-wracking. The goal is to create a performance that will capture the imagination of a filmmaker and their audience. This requires a great deal of focus from the actor, and it is crucial to be able to hit marks. It's important to be aware of the frame size, and it is helpful for actors with a theatre background to practice in front of a mirror and learn about the physicality of acting for the camera.

The actor also must be able to adjust to working with the sound track and music during the shoot. The music can distract the actor, and it can be difficult to maintain the energy needed for a solid take. It is recommended that the actor be well-rested and hydrated before beginning shooting. It is also a good idea to use the time between takes to stretch or engage in a workout. This will help the actor keep their energy up and prevent them from becoming distracted by the camera and director.

On-camera acting is also very different from stage acting in that the actor isn't presenting their performance to an audience. The camera is a magnifying glass that can reveal all the flaws and imperfections in a performance. This can be a little intimidating, but the actor can use it to their advantage by opening up and being vulnerable in front of the lens. This can lead to a more genuine and honest performance.

When the actor is on set, they should make sure that they are comfortable in their clothing and the lighting isn't too harsh. They should also avoid wearing anything that will wash out on screen, such as busy patterns or logos. Lastly, it's a good idea to bring water and snacks to the set to keep the actor hydrated and energized between takes.

While the differences between stage and camera acting can be overwhelming at first, it is a necessary part of an actor's career. Actors must embrace this difference and work hard to improve their craft. The result can be powerful and moving, creating performances that people will remember for decades to come. Just think of Monroe in Bus Stop, Bergman in Casablanca, Winslet in The Reader, McDormand in Three Billboards, or Lawrence in Winter's Bone. All of these performances were raw and honest, yet cheated in some way to create great cinema.

Working With the Camera

The camera essentially sees everything that is happening on screen. As actors, we are often asked to work within a specific frame, depending on what the director wants, whether it is a close-up or a wide shot. The key is to base your performance on the size of that frame, so you can create a sense of scale for yourself and your scene partner. Then, you can make your actions as big or small as the frame demands, rather than trying to impose your own ideas on the situation.

If you come from a theatre background, one of the most important things to remember is that there is no audience in front of you on set. You're performing for the crew and the director, not the viewing public. It's important to remember that and remember that the goal of your performance is to captivate those people, not the audience.

In television and film acting, you have to rely much more on your body language than in the theater. This is because you can't rely on the energy of the audience to carry you through the scene. Instead, you have to use the power of your eyes to connect with the audience and evoke an emotional response.

It's also important to be aware of the fact that the camera will pick up every little thing you do, which can include things that don't have much significance in the theater. For example, if an actor shrugs her eyebrows on stage, it may only be noticeable to the first few rows of the audience, but on camera that gesture can say everything you need to know about an emotional state.

In film and television, the camera is a very intimate tool, which can bring out a lot of raw honesty in a performance. But it can also lead to a great deal of cheating. The best performances, such as Monroe in Bus Stop, Bergman in Casablanca, Winslet in The Reader, McDormand in Three Billboards and Lawrence in Winter's Bone, are a mixture of raw honesty and the trickery and magic of cinema.

Subtlety of Performance

There's a common belief that stage acting has to be large and loud in order to reach the last row of a theater, while film acting is small and nuanced since the camera will catch every gesture. While this is true in a general sense, there are specific techniques that make for more effective performances when it comes to either type of acting.

For example, when it comes to a screen acting audition, if you're asked to shake your head or shrug your shoulders, it's important that you don't overdo it. The director wants to see you react to the imaginary situation that they've already created in their mind, so it's necessary to use your subtlety and control your gestures to convey the emotions that they're seeking.

Additionally, when speaking on camera it's important that you speak at a normal volume and not yell or whisper. You may also be asked to use your natural voice instead of a stage whisper, which can sound more lifelike and believable. If you're unsure what the director is looking for, ask them. They'll be happy to clarify what they want from you and will help you create the most effective performance.

While it's important to focus on your body language when you're performing for the camera, it's also essential that you work on your facial expressions as well. For example, the way you hold your eyebrows can convey a wide range of emotions and is something that is easy to transfer to screen acting. Practicing by putting different emotions on your face while you look at yourself in the mirror is an excellent way to build your skills and refine your technique.

Finally, it's important to eliminate any mannerisms that you might have in your daily life when you're acting for the camera. This can include things like flaring nostrils, touching your nose, crossing your arms and sighing. All of these can seem unnatural on the screen and take away from your overall performance. Taking acting classes and watching as much film as you can is an excellent way to learn how to eliminate any bad habits and perform at your best when working with the camera.

The Business of Acting

The Business of Acting explores the facets that make the industry fascinating and challenging. From networking to marketing, embracing these concepts will help you create a plan and goals for your acting career.

Most people respect actors for choosing a tough path that pushes them to their emotional, physical and financial limits. But that doesn't mean they should be treated poorly for it.

Insight into the Industry

The film industry is a multifaceted environment that requires a combination of art, craft and business acumen to thrive. Whether you are an aspiring actor or working in the field, it is crucial to understand the intricacies of the industry to make informed career decisions and move forward.

Actors need to develop a clear understanding of the business of acting, including how to land agents, impress casting directors and book jobs. This will help them set realistic goals and plan for their future careers. In addition, knowing how to market themselves effectively will give actors an edge over their competition.

It is also important for actors to know how to navigate contracts and negotiations. This is because the industry can be highly unpredictable, and it is not uncommon for actors to go long periods of time without work. Being familiar with industry standards and seeking legal advice can empower actors to navigate these challenges successfully.

Another important aspect of the business of acting is financial planning. It is essential for actors to budget their expenses and save money. This will ensure financial stability and security throughout their careers. It is also a good idea to diversify income streams, such as by teaching acting classes or taking on voice-over work.

It is also important for actors to network with other professionals in the industry. This can be done through social media platforms such as Instagram, TikTok and Twitter. By posting behind-the-scenes footage, sharing personal insights and engaging with fans, actors can establish their brand and connect with potential clients. In addition, attending acting school can provide an excellent networking opportunity, as it often features guest lectures and workshops from industry professionals who are willing to share their experiences.

Getting an Agent

One of the most important aspects of being an actor is knowing how to market yourself. Getting an agent is an essential part of this, and they can help you get jobs that would otherwise be unavailable. In addition, a good agent can provide advice and guidance on acting techniques. They can also help you develop a portfolio and reel.

The first step to becoming an actor is to build a strong resume through theater performances, student films and independent projects. Once you've built up a portfolio, you can begin looking for agents who can represent you. It's best to find an agent who specializes in the type of work you want to do. It's also helpful to network with other actors, as they can offer you insight into the industry and give you tips on how to improve your acting skills.

Many people who pursue a career as an actor struggle to stay in the industry because it's so difficult and competitive. It's also a risky business, and if you can't cope with the rejection and instability, it's best to look for a different career path.

In order to be a successful actor, you need to take the business seriously. It's important to have a strong foundation of training and experience, and to be ready to accept constructive criticism and advice from industry professionals. It's also important to practice sound financial management so that you can sustain your acting career and make it last as long as possible.

The most important thing to remember is that you have a passion for acting, and it's something that makes you happy. If you're able to tolerate the rigours of the industry and put in the hard work, you'll be well on your way to becoming a professional actor!

Joining Unions

Unions have helped make important advances in workplace rights, including the minimum wage, social security payments, an eight hour workday and weekends, overtime pay, and worker safety standards. According to UC Berkeley Labor Center, workers in unions are more likely to be satisfied with their jobs and more productive on the job.

Many acting schools provide networking opportunities with professionals from a variety of domains in the film industry. Guest lectures, workshops and industry-focused events are also frequently organized. Students should take advantage of these opportunities to learn from other actors, directors, producers and members of the film crew.

Actors should focus on perfecting their craft and developing their acting skills. They must be able to express emotion, remain in character and translate words on the page into an experience for an audience. They must also be able to communicate with the director, producer and other cast and crew members. Strong communication skills are essential in order to prevent delays, adhere to budgets, and ensure that everyone understands the creative vision of the film.

For those interested in becoming a professional actor, it is recommended that they enroll in a four-year school whose curriculum includes both acting classes and business education. This will give them the foundation needed to pursue a career in the industry.

Recent trends in the labor market suggest that unions may be regaining some popularity. A survey conducted by the talent platform Jobcase found that 41% of skilled and hourly workers are more likely to consider joining a union than they were 3 years ago. Meanwhile, a Pew Research Center poll suggests that 58% of Americans think that the decline in union participation has been bad for working people.

Headshots

Whether you're just getting started as an actor or you've been in the industry for years, you can't go very far without having some great acting headshots. Headshots are the professional calling cards of actors and the first thing casting directors see when they look at you. A good headshot conveys your general age range, your possible occupations, your character archetypes, your professionalism and even hints at your inner emotional life.

While you can have amateur headshots taken on your phone, the best way to get great acting headshots is to find a reputable photographer who specializes in creating headshots for actors. They know how to position you in ways that will highlight your best features and create a headshot that will look professional. Additionally, a professional photographer will have the proper equipment and software to properly edit and retouch your images so they look their best.

When choosing a photographer to shoot your headshots, be sure to research them and see the work they've done for other clients. It's also helpful to have an idea of what type of headshot you want. For example, if you're looking to become a television presenter you'll want to have some images that are more formal and professional while someone who wants to do commercial acting will need some headshots that are more relaxed and friendly.

Headshots are traditionally printed in an 8"x10" format. They can be printed in black and white or color. Most actors prefer to have their headshots printed in color since it's more intuitive for a casting director to flip the headshot over and read the actor's resume on the back. Photographers use either studio lighting or natural light to capture their subject's image.

Resumes

As an aspiring actor, you need to build professional experience by auditioning and landing roles. Keeping your resume and headshot up-to-date is an important part of this process. This also means making sure that you have these documents available to show casting directors, producers and other industry professionals when networking.

The first thing you need to do when creating a resume is decide on a format. There are three popular choices: chronological, functional and hybrid. Chronological is a great choice if you have a solid work history in your field of interest and are looking for a similar position. A functional resume organizes your experiences based on skill, which is good if you are changing careers or lack direct work experience in your new field. A hybrid is a combination of both formats and is the most flexible. When choosing a format, keep in mind that hiring managers have short attention spans. Brevity, a clean layout and concise language are prized by employers.

When describing your career experience, use action words like "achieved," "designed," "improved" and "maintained." Avoid generic phrases, such as "hard worker" or "team player." Employers want to know what you have done, so be specific.

Include a summary at the top of your resume that includes your main accomplishments and skills. Also, provide a list of relevant education. You should include the name of the school, your degree and major and minor, the month and year you graduated and your GPA. Finally, include any honors and awards you have received. These can help you stand out from the competition. When writing your resume, be sure to optimize it for applicant tracking systems (ATS). These are computer software programs that companies use to sort and select job applicants. Hiring managers search ATS databases for keywords that appear in the job description they are looking to fill. Those who use ATS-optimized resumes are more likely to be selected for an interview than those who do not.

Self-Care For Actors

Performing can be strenuous, physically and emotionally. From long rehearsals to tech week and performances, it can take its toll on actors.

Taking care of yourself will help you be your best and stay in the game longer. Learn some simple tips to improve your self-care.

Mental Health

A career as an actor can be extremely rewarding, but it is also incredibly stressful. With long hours on set, rejection, and being in the public eye all the time, it can take a toll on an actor's mental health. Having a good support system and a balance between work and personal life are essential for actors to maintain their well-being.

Many actors find their passion in acting, and see it as a calling that they couldn't imagine doing anything else. They feel that the craft helps them to grow and develop as individuals, and they often feel like they're a better person for it. Unfortunately, that can come with a number of challenges as well. The stress of the profession can lead to anxiety and depression, which are common mental health issues.

Research into the connection between acting and mental health is scant, but there are a few projects that aim to bridge that gap. Actor Alice Brockway is working on a PhD on the topic, and has created the website Playing Sane as a space for people in the industry to discuss their experiences openly. The coronavirus pandemic has also shed light on the fact that entertainment industry workers, specifically those working behind the scenes, tend to experience mental health challenges more frequently than others, and that they're often not easily able to access services.

It's important for actors to know the signs and symptoms of mental health issues so that they can seek help when needed. They should also be able to recognise when they're feeling burnt out or over-stressed, and learn ways to manage those feelings.

One way to do this is by ensuring that they have a healthy and balanced diet, as well as getting enough sleep each night. It's also a good idea to get some exercise, as this can help to reduce stress and increase happiness.

Additionally, it's important for actors to have a positive and supportive social network, which can provide them with an emotional outlet when they need it. They should also try to spend some time away from their work, so that they can recharge and feel energized when they return to it.

The study also found that about 80 percent of the respondents were active users of legal and illegal drugs, which was likely a result of the various stresses of being an actor, such as financial pressure, 'stage fright', bullying, and sexual harassment. The use of substances to self-medicate was an attempt to deal with these problems, which can be incredibly difficult for actors to cope with. The study also revealed that many actors felt that their work peaked by the age of 30. Some had difficulty 'shaking off' the intense emotions and physical demands of their roles, even after the project was finished.

Physical Wellness

Actors are not only responsible for learning their lines and ensuring they look the part, but also for keeping themselves healthy. The acting industry can be physically demanding on an actor's body, making it crucial to have a good exercise regimen and maintain a balanced diet. These habits can not only boost an actor's overall health, but also help them achieve a more authentic and realistic performance.

When preparing for a role, actors can use breathing exercises to calm their nerves and reduce feelings of anxiety. The physical activity can also help them keep their heart rate down, which in turn will make it easier for them to focus on the task at hand. Actors are also encouraged to stretch and flex their muscles before performing, as this can help them prepare for the demands of the scene.

Stress can be a major obstacle for actors, and can impact their mental health and physical appearance. When a performer is stressed, their cortisol levels increase, which can interfere with their ability to remember their lines and blocking. It can also cause their muscles to tighten and lead to stiffness and pain. It's important for actors to work on stress reduction techniques, like meditation and yoga, so that they can keep their mental clarity and remain healthy.

Another way that actors can maintain their wellness is by having a support system of fellow actors who understand the struggles of the business. The support of a community can help them manage the emotional toll of being undervalued as an actor and help them stay grounded and happy in their careers.

Actors can also prioritize their well-being by learning to say no when necessary. It's easy to become overwhelmed by commitments, especially when you have a busy schedule, so it's important to learn how to set boundaries for yourself and take time out for yourself. This can be as simple as scheduling a weekly massage or booking an afternoon of Netflix and chill, to taking a yoga class and staying in to read a book.

Practicing self-care doesn't have to be difficult, and actors should start small and be patient. Many times, it takes a few attempts before something sticks. Once an actor finds a routine they enjoy and are able to stick with it, they should then set goals for themselves to grow their wellness even further. This can be as simple as eating healthier, working out more, or simply making sure to drink enough water. As long as you're making an effort, you'll see the rewards.

Maintaining a Balanced Life

In the acting industry, we often hear terms like "tough, thick skinned" and "being a actor requires immense bravery and grit." These qualities are absolutely essential to being a successful actor, but they can be dangerous if not kept in check. If you spend too much time focused on building a strong career, your health and mental wellness can suffer. Here are a few tips for maintaining balance in your life, so you can continue to thrive as an actor!

Getting enough sleep. Performing can be exhausting, so it's important to get adequate rest to prepare for your next show or audition. It may be difficult to do this during rehearsals and long shoot days, but try your best to prioritize sleep as much as possible. It'll help to prevent unsightly dark circles under your eyes and keep you feeling energetic.

Talking to someone about your feelings. Actors are no stranger to stress, and it's always a good idea to have people to talk with who can relate. Friends and family can provide support, but if you want to have a more professional relationship, consider a counselor or coach. They'll be able to offer you guidance and perspective on your career, as well as personal issues that are impacting you.

Finding a hobby that makes you happy outside of the acting industry. You can take up a new sport, learn a language, or find another creative outlet that allows you to step out of your actor brain for a while. This can help you feel more grounded and will also make you a more interesting person to be around.

Remember that it's okay to fail. It's a learning experience, and it will help you become a better actor. Don't be afraid to try new things, but don't let perfectionism stop you from pursuing your dreams.

Keeping these simple self-care habits in mind can be the difference between booking that role and going home empty handed. With a little bit of attention and care, you'll be ready to take on your career and give it the best shot. Good luck!

The Evolution of an Actor

Research has shown that highly empathic individuals are drawn to acting. Researchers believe that this is because actors often experience their character's life circumstances without any evaluative judgment.

Konstantin Stanislavski developed a series of training techniques to help actors develop natural performances. These are now known as the Stanislavsky method.

Evolution of a Career

An actor's career is often volatile and unpredictable, with plenty of ups and downs. This is especially true for those trying to establish themselves in the industry. Aspiring actors must be prepared for years of auditions, rejection and bit parts before landing a role they can call their own. Then there's the rest of their life; the profession can mean considerable time away from family and friends as well as regular disruption to the routine of daily living.

It's important that people hoping to become actors do their research into training options before making a decision. Actors should look for reputable institutions that have an excellent track record and are recommended by peers. They should also take the opportunity to learn from other industry professionals by attending workshops, master classes and lectures. It's also worth checking that the institution is a member of an arts union as this can help protect actors from exploitation.

Actors can spend a significant amount of their careers moving between theatre, radio and television. They may find themselves performing roles that are similar to each other with no progression or pay rise and it can be easy for them to feel typecast into a certain style of performance.

But every now and then a role comes along that completely shatters expectations and sends the actor on a new trajectory, repositioning them as a different kind of performer.

In addition to acting work, some actors also branch out into other areas of entertainment such as writing, directing and stand-up comedy. As artists, they tend to have a highly creative and cultural lifestyle that can be very fulfilling. They are often very well-read and have a deep understanding of history and culture.

Many actors also spend a considerable amount of their working life travelling across the country and sometimes the world to audition for roles. This can be very disruptive to their home and personal lives and it's important that they have good relationships with their families, who may be understandably upset by the amount of time they are spending away from them. It's also worthwhile for people in this industry to join a union, which can not only protect them from exploitation but can also help them with financial security and access to professional support services.

The Challenges

In addition to the physical and emotional demands of the profession, actors must also work hard at marketing themselves. This involves building relationships with agents, directors, and producers; the creative industry is a small place where reputation can make or kill careers faster than any missed opportunity or bad performance. Actors must be able to network effectively and keep up with the latest trends in their field to stay relevant and ensure they are working on projects that are interesting and rewarding.

Actors are often required to travel a great deal in order to secure roles, especially for those who want to remain in film and television. This can mean that they spend a significant amount of time away from family and friends. It can be difficult to balance a career as an actor with the demands of other aspects of life, such as paying bills or maintaining social relationships. The constant travelling can be exhausting and lead to a lack of stability in one's lifestyle, which is a challenge that many actors struggle with.

Although there are a number of challenges associated with the career, there is no denying that acting can be incredibly rewarding and fulfilling. The most important thing for any aspiring actor is to understand that it will take time and effort before they can achieve success. As a result, they should be prepared for the inevitable downtimes that will occur in their career and try to remain positive about these periods.

For those who are already committed to the profession, it is important to stay focused and remember that there are plenty of people out there who will always be interested in what they have to say. For this reason, it is essential to maintain a positive attitude and be proud of your achievements to date, regardless of whether they are big or small.

There is a growing interest in understanding how psychological attributes such as personality traits and creativity might differentiate professional actors from other types of workers. Fortunately, several existing studies have collected impressive sample sizes to date; however, most of these studies have relied on traditional mean-comparison or ordinary least square predictive methods.

Stay Relevant

Staying relevant and inspired over time is a challenge in any industry, but it's particularly critical for actors. It's important to find ways to reimagine your brand and better serve your existing clients, while also anticipating the needs of future customers.

One way to do this is by creating your own work. Many of today's most exciting new actors started out by creating their own web series, like Rachel Bloom ("Crazy Ex-Girlfriend") and Issa Rae and Abbi Jacobson ("Broad City"). By doing so, they were able to develop their craft and find their audience.

Inspiration

An actor needs to be able to take inspiration from a variety of sources. They may find ideas from a book, poem or other work of art. They can also find inspiration from a person or experience that has affected their life in some way. The most successful actors are able to create characters that are unique and authentic to them.

This can be achieved through the practice of Method acting, which was developed by Lee Strasberg. This approach focuses on finding deep resources of imagination and sensitivity that can be used as the basis for (re)experiencing a character in performance. Actors have been doing this instinctively for centuries, but prior to the work of Stanislavsky and Strasberg there was no system for training the faculties required to deliver truly inspired performances.

A central concept of Method acting is that the actor must be able to re-experience the character on stage, film or television as though it was actually occurring in real time. This is done by relying on a highly sensitive faculty called affective memory, which allows the actor to consciously draw upon genuine emotions that have already been experienced in their life.

To achieve this, the actor must be able to transform physically and emotionally into their character. This requires hard work, technique and good direction. Many method actors will even refuse to break character until the final scene of a film or their last performance of a play, often changing sleeping and eating habits to do so.

If an actor is not able to be fully inspired during a performance, they will lack depth and realism. This is why the process of preparing for a role is so important. This helps the actor become more receptive to inspiration, which is crucial for creating the right character.

Ultimately, an actor will need to have the ability to adapt to their environment and their audience. This means that they must be able to switch between modes, from being passionate and emotional to being cool and calm. This is not easy, but it is essential if an actor is to be successful.

Conclusion

In the journey through the art of acting, we've traversed a rich landscape of history, technique, and personal evolution. Our exploration began with the roots of acting, tracing its lineage from the ancient amphitheaters to the dynamic stages and screens of today. We delved into the actor's instrument—body and voice—uncovering ways to hone these tools through discipline and care.

The chapters on acting techniques unveiled the tapestry of methodologies that have shaped the craft. From Stanislavski to Meisner, we explored the philosophies and practices that enable actors to breathe authentic life into their characters. Character development emerged as a cornerstone of our discussion, a process where research and imagination intertwine to create memorable and believable personas.

We ventured into the realm of script analysis, equipping actors with the skills to dissect texts and unearth the nuances of story and character. Improvisation, we discovered, is not merely an exercise but a vital skill that fosters spontaneity and inventive thinking.

The rehearsal process, often veiled from public view, was demystified, revealing the collaborative heartbeat that pulses behind the scenes. Here, the symbiotic relationship between actor and director comes to life, shaping performances that captivate audiences.

Voice and diction, alongside physicality and movement, form the expressive palette from which actors paint their performances. These chapters emphasized the significance of clear speech, nuanced voice modulation, and the eloquent use of the body in storytelling.

We then turned inward, examining the emotional life of an actor. The chapters highlighted the delicate balance between accessing deep emotions for a role and maintaining psychological well-being. The craft of acting, as we've seen, demands not only talent but also emotional resilience.

Audition techniques offered practical guidance, demystifying the process and providing strategies to stand out in a competitive industry. Transitioning from stage to screen, we addressed the unique demands of acting for the camera, underscoring the subtleties that distinguish a compelling on-screen performance.

The business of acting brought to light the industry's realities—navigating agents, unions, and the intricacies of building a sustainable career. In this realm, tenacity and adaptability emerged as indispensable traits.

Our penultimate focus on self-care for actors served as a reminder that amidst the rigors of the profession, maintaining mental and physical health is paramount. The industry's pressures are real, and nurturing one's well-being is not a luxury but a necessity.

Finally, we contemplated the evolution of an actor, a journey marked by continuous growth, learning, and adaptation. The actor's path is one of perpetual reinvention, where each role, each performance, is an opportunity for transformation.

In concluding, the craft of acting is a mosaic of history, technique, emotion, and relentless pursuit of authenticity. It's an art that demands not only talent but an unwavering commitment to the craft. This book aimed to provide a compass for navigating the multifaceted world of acting—a guide for those aspiring to the heights of this venerable art and a reflection for the seasoned artist. Acting, at its core, is a journey into the human experience, an endeavor that mirrors life in its complexity, beauty, and ceaseless evolution.

Don't miss out!

Visit the website below and you can sign up to receive emails whenever Lloyd Green publishes a new book. There's no charge and no obligation.

https://books2read.com/r/B-A-RYABB-CHHQC

Did you love *The Essence of Acting: Techniques, Triumphs, and Trials*?
Then you should read *Legends of the Diamond: The New York Yankees'
Timeless Tale*[1] by Lloyd Green!

[2]

Dive into the illustrious saga of America's most iconic baseball team
with "Legends of the Diamond: The New York Yankees' Timeless Tale."
This comprehensive chronicle is a must-have addition to any baseball
aficionado's library, offering an unparalleled journey through the
storied history of the New York Yankees.

Spanning over a century of baseball magic, "Legends of the
Diamond" captures the essence of the Yankees' legacy. From the early
days of the Highlanders to the dynasty years and the modern-era
triumphs, this book brings to life the extraordinary narratives that

---

1. https://books2read.com/u/m26L6r

2. https://books2read.com/u/m26L6r

have cemented the Yankees as a symbol of resilience, excellence, and community.

Packed with New York Yankees trivia, this treasure trove of information will satisfy the most ardent fans and curious newcomers alike. Discover fun facts about Yankee greats, iconic games, and pivotal moments that shaped the franchise. Each page is a celebration of the legends who donned the pinstripes, turning baseball into a spectacle of heroics and heart.

Beyond the on-field exploits, "Legends of the Diamond" delves into the Yankees' commitment to philanthropy, chronicling their extensive community work and impact beyond the ballpark. It's a testament to the team's understanding of their role as stewards of the public trust, making it not only a captivating read but also an inspiring one.

Beautifully written and meticulously researched, this book is more than just a history; it's a homage to a team that has become synonymous with the sport of baseball. Whether you're looking for the perfect New York Yankees gift for the die-hard fan in your life or seeking to enrich your own understanding of this legendary team, "Legends of the Diamond" is a grand slam.

So, step up to the plate and immerse yourself in the timeless tale of the New York Yankees, where every chapter is an inning in an epic game that continues to captivate the world. "Legends of the Diamond" is not just a recounting of the past; it's an invitation to be a part of the ongoing legacy of the most storied franchise in baseball history.

Also by Lloyd Green

The Prepper's Ultimate Guide: Building Sustainable Shelters for
Long-Term Survival
Original Six Era: The Rise of the Chicago Blackhawks Dynasty
Legends of the Diamond: The New York Yankees' Timeless Tale
The First Kiss Blueprint: Steps to a Moment She'll Never Forget
The Essence of Acting: Techniques, Triumphs, and Trials

www.ingramcontent.com/pod-product-compliance
Lightning Source LLC
Chambersburg PA
CBHW061328120726
48001CB00002B/744